I would lik

To the countless men and women of the Peshmerga,

Who have valiantly died by the hundreds and thousands

In the past and to this day for my Beloved Kurdistan

From terrorism and for Freedom…

-

To Masoud Barzani, President of Iraqi Kurdistan,

Whose dream and vison for a united Kurdistan

And continued struggle to promote peace

Has my deepest and most sincere respect…

-

To the many American soldiers who helped dispose

A most cruel dictator that eradicated so many of us Kurds

And all those allies who overthrew such a regime of hatred

You are all in my undying debt…

-

And to my father, the man I aspire to be

May you rest in peace.

May Allah bless you as He has blessed me.

Introduction

This little book aims to do two things. There is the obvious first, which is to tell a story about a Kurdish refugee. Of course, this action can be accomplished by many people and really provides no prominence in the vast repertoire of biographies to which anyone can choose amongst the nearest bookstores. Everyone has a story and many have written theirs, but a great biography stands out among those others in part because there is a real purpose in what it intends to say. Many people who write their own stories do so for many different reasons-stemming all the way from pure vanity to a willingness to help someone to understand an author-and a great biography is determined by an audience who analyzes the very impact that knowledge has upon them and others.

When I questioned Shawket why he wanted to write a memoir about himself, I soon discovered a very interesting answer. Whenever he spoke, he seemed to speak for the vast majority of people that he himself identifies with. For this reason, I realized that he wanted his story to be written so that others might know of the Kurds, and their struggles and culture. His story is their story. This is why he wanted his story written, which is an interesting thing to think about honestly. Who wants to write a story about himself to reflect about his people? Perhaps this is all Shawket knows, and the only way he can connect with his people. However, he has continuously made the point that his people are left unnoticed, both from history and from acknowledgement of their achievements in the modern world today. It has certainly been something he has truly wanted to change. In helping write his story, I realize my job was to carry this message across throughout his book, to showcase his desire to make known to the audience of the Kurdish people, long forgotten in the pages of history and violence.

Thus, writing Shawket's story is primarily to write a Kurdish story, one that Kurdish people can understand and relate to, and to which a wider audience can experience and acknowledge. It took me a long time to come to understand this very simple aspect of Shawket, however, it is definitely a character that must be deeply accessed, for his story is a serious story, one that grips to the very grim reality of a people who are constantly in conflict with themselves and those around them. His story is a constant reflection of the Kurdish culture and their way of doing things. Thus, sometimes is it helpful to think of Shawket's life as that of any typical refugee, keeping in mind the struggles of a person who had to flee his homeland, struggle to survive, and still identify with him or herself while having to start over again with practically nothing.

Co-authoring this short memoir was both an interesting and rewarding task. After hundreds of pages of text, we narrowed down this short book to what it is today. We tried writing in almost every way possible. For a while, we couldn't decide whether to make this book into a short biography or historical text with personal views on the events that occurred in Kurdistan. However, we both felt that it would be much more effective to make this book from a personal view, because it captured Shawket in its fullest form. Thus, Shawket wrote the text and I edited the script, since I had a better understanding of the English language and grammar than he did. I studied the Kurdish history and helped incorporate this into his story so as to put things in perspective. We worked together on this project for two years, contacting each other and drinking many liters of tea along the way. In the end, we finally came to feel confident in what is now the current book you are holding.

In retrospect, it was not possible for me to completely get a perfect picture of Shawket and his story. After all, I am no expert in English literature, and surely lack any experience in writing peer-reviewed papers. I am an amateur writer, experienced in writing countless papers often left unedited and forgotten under hundreds of papers over random thoughts, ideas, stories, poems, and memoiric and philosophical musings. Thus, I must apologize for my imperfections, my haste, my questions that may not have covered all the possible grounds to which an audience may desire to know the answers to, and the complete understanding of a culture that seems as foreign to me as to anyone who may never have heard of or ever seen it. It is, however, my hope that the effort that I did put into Shawket's story, and that of his people, will be appreciated and my shortcomings overlooked, at least professionally, because the point of this book is not to be academically correct but rather to tell a story that represents a much larger idea than what is pictured. I hope that the Kurdish people come to understand my foreign perspective in such a vibrant and wholly interesting culture, and be proud that a bit of their story was able to be represented to the world. If this outcome is successful, I feel that I shall have accomplished my obligation to their culture and Shawket.

Finally, I want to thank Shawket for asking me to take this immense task. It is truly an honor when a person trusts another to help them relate their story to others. Besides being a good friend, he has been a constant support for me and my understanding of his culture. I must give him all the credit for this book because he took the time to relate and write numerous notes about it to me many times, while also constantly reminding me when I started procrastinating. I want to thank his wife, Fatima, for allowing me into their home, and cooking so many amazing foods and making the best Kurdish tea I've ever tasted, enabling me to experience a very important part of Kurdish culture. My sincere thanks goes out to all the people who helped make this story on paper a reality. Books are never easy to create and publish, and it takes many dedicated people to get them from paper to actual books. Finally, I want to acknowledge the Kurdish people. Although much befalls them and much happens towards them and around them, this book is dedicated to you. Many times, when a people speak, their voices can often be consumed and swallowed by a force so much larger and greater than themselves, but this doesn't mean that a people's voice and existence doesn't exist. In fact, it only implies the opposite. One must cross the obstacle and try to hear what is difficult to hear. For you, Kurdistan, you are truly the voices over the mountains.

Nicolae Viorel Burcea

Editor

Chapter One

Orman

I grew up in Kurdistan, in the village of Orman. I don't remember too well how it looked when I was there, because I was there only briefly. But I was told by my family what it was like. They said that beyond the village were many hills rolling with dark green grass. It was peaceful and silent, far away from the world of violence that I would later come to see. It is famous, you know, for its fruits. Every hill had a fruit, whether apple or grape, rolling like a dotted Persian rug through the hills and pastures. Orman is also famous for its nuts. Down the very heart of the village runs a main street with houses on each side. Mountains protect the village on either side, and it is very close to the country of Turkey. This is where I was born. This is the beginning.

Orman in the 1960s, before I was born. This is an extremely rare photo of my mother's parents' home.

My family name is *Barwary,* and we lived in the district of Barwarybala, about 75 villages, living close to the mountains. The Barwarybala people are comparable to a small tribe, one very closely knitted. We lived almost exclusively in the mountains, and for this reason, the people who were fighting the Saddam Hussein regime would escape to the mountains and would only come down to the villages for medical treatment or for food and supplies. At the time, the government was not aware this was happening because the mountains were a refuge from the regime. As Kurds, whenever something happened, we fled towards the mountains, for this was our home, our turf, and no one could beat us from our land.

We Kurds are all like family, and my family in particular is highly respected amongst the people of the land. My father won the respect of the people because he was a very generous man. He was keen to please his guest, and to respect all that aspired to wish his service. His name was Abdullah, and he was the nearby school's maintaince man. He had humble origins and a decent job, but he was revered in Orman for his gift of peace. Whenever the villagers had any issue, whatever it might be, they asked my father to mediate the situation and help them compromise. My father was so good at doing this, that the people of the village came to respect him and his understanding and hospitality. It would be a virtue I would hold dear to myself and uphold for the rest of my life.

My father was so well known for his generosity that much later in life, when my brother went away to college in Erbil at the University of Salahaddin, he encountered an incident for which much praise must go to my father. One day, my brother was outside, trying to get a taxi to go shopping. When a taxi stopped, and both men exchanged salutations, the taxi driver noted that my brother spoke another dialect and was from Dahuk, which is a city in Kurdistan. After asking him several questions about what part of Dahuk he was from and what his family name was (my family name is *Qutats*), he abruptly stopped the car, got out, opened the door from my brother's side, pulled my brother out, and started hugging him and crying. When my brother, who was confused and scared, asked him what was happening, the driver said "Your father is my father. I was a teacher in your village. There was nothing that was needed that your father didn't provide for my family."

An extremely rare photo of my father, the man that inspires me even to this day. He is wearing the traditional Kurdish headdress. He died when I was barely a year old.

Also, my father was generous to guests. If anyone new appeared in the village, whether a stranger or family friend, he would rush out and take him home. He would even take his children's food to provide for the guests. He became famous for his hospitality and the ability to mediate issues in the village whenever they arose. I try to uphold this honor and respect that my father had, and I try not to let my family name down. My father worked hard to earn that respect and I don't want to ruin it by being foolish.

My father had two wives. The first one was *Asia*, who was my stepmother. She had five children, all of whom were my step siblings: *Taib, Aishan, Salah, Ramazan*, and *Shereen*. The second wife was my mother, *Rahema*, whose name means "mercy". She had five children as well: *Sabah, Nazerah, Adris, Fatima*, and me, Shawket. I was the youngest of everyone in the family, both from my father's first wife or my mother. This was my family, and they all lived in Orman before I was born, in 1977. Taib, my oldest brother and the oldest of my siblings, was 18 years older than me.

My father's situation was very good. He had a big house, two floors, and was much respected. In Kurdish culture, when one is well off, and respected, and has many guests, it is not forbidden to have more than one wife to help about the household and take care of the children and the guests. For this reason, my father married my mother, who was much younger, to help my stepmother and help each other take care of the children. Of course, this was possible because my father had the resources to maintain a large home and treat the wives fairly, which he did.

Now, the area of Kurdistan where Orman is located is in northern Iraq. At the time, in 1970s, Saddam Hussein was taking control of Iraq, and he was very much against the Kurds. He knew that we fought against his regime and took refuge in our mountains. It is for this reason that, one day, an incident occurred, and it changed our lives forever. What I know about this incident is what

I was told by my family and other people from the village.

I had uncles who were well known Kurdish fighters, and my father was providing everything for them whenever they came to Orman. And, within our village, there were several people who were secret spies for the Saddam Hussein government. One of them had made a plan with another person in Orman to kill my father, most possibly because my father was helping the Kurdish fighters who were going against the regime.

I was very young, too young to remember, what exactly happened. However, one evening, after my father came home from work at the school. I was crying, and he came inside and held me, and then started to play with me. He heard a noise outside that sounded like some kids fighting. One of my brothers and some kids apparently had gotten into a fight of some sort. However, my father did not know what was going on, so he went outside to see who was making the noise. While he was walking down the road towards the noise, one of the spies located himself on top of one of the buildings. He had a big rock, and when my father walked near where he was, he threw the rock right at his head. He must have hit him exactly at his head because my father died instantly.

So, the people of the village came together and found out who had done the act. Although my family tried very hard to prosecute the spy, it was useless because the regime would not try one of their own people who worked for them. My brothers and uncles wanted to fight back because my father was killed for no reason, however, nothing happened at that time. In my culture, when someone kills another for no reason, such action does not get unpunished and forgotten. For Kurds, it stays forever, and one day, whomever punishes will get punished.

Several years later, a regional election occurred in the city of Darkar, and one of my uncles was there to vote. The spy who had killed my father was also present, with about seven friends. So, my uncle, *Mohammed*, went to my oldest brother, *Taib*, and told him that my father's killer was at the election. At that time *Taib* had assumed my father's place as the head of the family, and there was an obligation on his part to make peace with our father's death. In our culture, when a person leaves his family's death unpunished, people say that they were afraid to act in their family's honor, which is disgraceful and weak. Thus, Taib and Mohammed decided that they would confront the killer and avenge my father.

So, my brother and uncle confronted the man who had killed my father. They started yelling at the killer, and the man suddenly realized who they were. A fight broke out, and my brother, who simply did not care about losing his life to avenge my father, killed the man's brother, injured three or four of his other brothers and cousins, and injured the killer by stabbing him in the neck. My brother and uncle and others had a terrible confrontation.

When authority arrived, everyone was sent to the hospital and then prison for several months. The government assessed the situation as a family feud and would not interfere too much over the incident. To them, it seemed like a better option because the feud could continue, and would lead into more conflict and more death, which was ideal for them because they clearly hated us Kurds and wanted us to fight and die amongst ourselves. However, later on, one of the prominent *Barwary* leaders came around and settled the issue between both families. Today, they live in the same city, and although they don't meet each other, they attend the same funerals and ceremonies. I tell this story not to harm their goodwill but to explain how my father got killed and how that issue was resolved. Needless to say, today, we are respectable friends and we mean no hard towards one another.

Later, some of my brothers went to the mountains and fought for the *Peshmergha,* which is the main group of Kurdish freedom fighters. My brother *Sabah* became the leader of the house, and took his role in raising *Taib's* children and my siblings. However, things did not fare well, for Saddam Hussein took his wrath on all the Kurds and eradicated all their homes and villages by bulldozing them to the ground and relocated them. This is what happened in Orman, to my village.

In 1978/1979, the Iraqi government sent troops in Orman and relocated my family and all the Kurds in the village. They relocated us to a nearby compound village called Darkar. It was around this time that my brother asked my mother to remarry, but, she refused. She said that she did not want me to grow up with a father that was not my own; thus, she was not going to marry again. She became ill at this time as well, because of the stress and the anxiety of what was happening at the time.

I really don't remember Orman. I was a baby when all these things took place. As such, all that I have recollected are things I have heard from my family and others. However, this new city, Darkar, I would come to know very well, for it is here that I really and truly grew up. It is essentially where my life as a Kurd begins and where I can remember what happened. Orman is important because it was a Kurdish village, left by itself in its beautiful surroundings. It was our land, our mountains, our fruit, our lives, our home. It was everything to us before it was all taken away and we were sent to Darkar.

Orman today. Nowadays, Orman is a small and peaceful village, as it was before the Iraqi regime came and relocated us to Darkar.

Chapter 2

Darkar

The 1980s and 1990s saw the Middle East in much turmoil, and for us Kurds, exceptionally so. Many of the Kurdish villages, towns, and farms were rampaged, and the people were sent to government-made compounds, or relocation camps. After the military raided our villages and homes, we were rounded up and taken to a nearby town called Darkar. It was closer to the nearby city but farther away from the border, so that the Iraqi government could supervise everything that we did. Because all of our belongings were taken away, when we left Orman and came to Darkar, we all had to start from nothing.

My house in Darkar, where we were relocated to. Notice the common layout and architecture of the building. All the houses in Darkar looked about the same.

Darkar was neither modern nor unique. The houses were similar. Indeed, they were compounds. There was a big road that went right through the village, and the tan stone shone in the hot sun, reminding us every day that this wasn't our home but that we were prisoners in a foreign territory. Everything looked and felt military, and there was a tense atmosphere in the air whenever anyone walked in Darkr. There was a Ba'ath Party[1] headquarters in the village, as well as an Iraqi police station. There was a small hospital, as well as two elementary schools, one for boys and one for girls. There was also a middle school up to 9th grade, and after that we went to the nearby city high school.

The elementary school I attended. Notice the Kurdish flag on the post. When I lived there, this school flew the Iraqi flag.

The Iraqi government dictated a great deal of what we could and could not do. I was sent to school, but I was taught in the Arabic language, except for one Kurdish class, which was difficult because it was in another Kurdish dialect, Sorani, that was difficult to learn because it was different from our Bahdenani dialect. I only spoke my language with my family and friends, who were also Kurds. I recall that we didn't have school on Friday, but every Thursday, we had to put on a uniform that symbolized the Ba'ath Party and go to the nearby school park, where we sang the Iraqi national anthem whether we wanted to or not. The intelligence in the village was rather scary because you clearly could tell who was loyal to whom. It was clear that to rebuke the regime was to rebuke yourself, your family, and possibly your life.

My brother supported us for a little while when he was in the army; however, he did not want to fight, so he purposely bruised himself by burning his leg so that he could be sent back home with us. My mother would pick plants and berries far in the mountains and sell them at the market in the city. I would go along with her when I could walk, helping her pick fruit from the trees and bushes. The water in Darkar was quite awful. We never seemed to have enough of it and it tasted terrible. There was a communal water area, but it took a long time to get it and haul it back home. It was a hard living. Perhaps the worst part of it all was the idea that the Arab people were in charge, telling is what to do. There was nothing we could do but comply and try to live out a normal life the only way we knew we could. Actually, we lived like prisoners.

It was in the Darkar that I grew up. I went to high school by government shuttles, to the nearest city Zakho, which was about a half hour away. I was always a top student, and I have always been proud of that. My favorite class was English. For some reason, I was fascinated with the English language, and knowing this language really helped me in my future life. There were days that I recall the teacher coming in and telling us we were going to have an extra class. He would ask the class which subject we wanted, and I was the only one who would choose English, whereas everyone else would choose a different topic. I joined the local football team and we won the championship in our area. I played football so much that I got a beating for getting my socks dirty every day. So, I would hide my socks so that my family wouldn't know I had played that day. Even today, I am a huge football fan of Real Madrid, which most likely stems from when I was a child playing in the streets and muddy pitches. I also played marbles, for this was a popular sport in Darkr. It was in my time in Darkar that Sabah, my oldest brother, got married in front of our house. It was also around this period that the incident between my uncle Mohammad and my brother occurred with the man who killed my father. It was also then that my sister, *Shereen*. She had a seizure while fetching water and she drowned. A lot happened from the time I arrived from Orman and grew up in Darkar. Back home, I was told we had everything, but in Darkar, we had to start from zero. I would go barefoot many times because we could not afford to buy shoes. What little we got monetarily was spent on what we absolutely needed and rarely did we ever buy anything we simply desired. However, most of these things I remember very briefly, and they don't seem to be that important since I consider them to be relatively normal in the realm of life. We tried to go about life the best way we could, and so we adapted to the situations and went about our business.

A piece of Kurdish culture, these "rollers" is what we used to pave our roofs to prevent water from seeping through.

However, while all this was occurring in Darkar, many other things were occurring in the Middle East. There were the Gulf Wars, and there were the accusations by the Iraqi government that the Kurds were helping the Iranian government. As a result, hundreds and thousands of Kurds were targeted and killed. Because there were wars going on, and Kurds were living on the borders between Iran and Iraq, we were often the first to die, and, as such, thousands of Kurdish people were killed. In the end, both Iran and Iraq agreed to find a way to diminish the Kurds. Iraq started using chemical weapons to kill Kurdish people, and, in one particular incident, in 1988, called the Halabja, they managed to massacre 5,000 Kurds, even though the regime denied that they had done it. In Barzan, the military surrounded the town, took all males, took them south, and buried them alive. That was about 8,000 Kurds. Since 2003, people have uncovered the bones of those Kurds but found it difficult to identify exactly who the individuals were. Many things were happening and many Kurds were targeted.

Meanwhile, while Saddam Hussein was enacting his own plans and being derailed by the Gulf Wars, the Kurds rose and started fighting for freedom. It was amazing because when we Kurds came together, nothing could stop us. We managed to liberate all of Kurdistan, Iraqi Kurdistan more specifically, and for a brief moment, in time the Kurdish people could breathe easy. Even though we were able to take back our land, we did not kill the Iraqi soldiers as they had killed us. Instead, we treated them more humanly, and I think this shows how much we respected ourselves and clearly didn't want conflict but rather celebration. We were aware that these Iraqi soldiers had families, wives and kids who were waiting for them and depending on them. So, we let them go, to Mosul. Big celebrations spread throughout the land, and in my village, Darkar, thousands of Iraqi soldiers were marched through our main street. To me, this was amazing. Suddenly, we could be ourselves-our own people. We could speak our own language and do what we wanted to do without having soldiers and enforcement around telling us what we could and could not do. It was a very proud moment, and I recall the celebrations lasting for months.

But, alas! Nothing lasts forever. For we were only independent for less than a year before Saddam Hussein threatened us Kurds by using chemical weapons. The soldiers we had left in Mosul were armed again and told to come after us Kurds and kill us. I guess it comes as no surprise. This was the same man that would try to occupy Kuwait and have almost the whole world go to war against him. Needless to say, Kuwait was very far away from us, and we didn't have a world coalition come to our aid. If the Iraqi soldiers came for us, we would have surely been killed or something as bad. Therefore, a radio announcement was sent out by the Iraqi regime, letting us Kurds know that the soldiers were coming. I'm not sure what was coming, and we never stayed to find out. People in Darkar left everything. My family left everything. That early morning, we ran. We ran and we ran. We found a tractor, and we all got on and sped away. We rode until it ran out of fuel, and we ran again. We ran and we ran. For the mountains. For the border. For our lives.

[1] The Ba'ath Party is a political party founded in Syria that ideologically promotes Arab nationalism and pan-Arabism. At the time that I was growing up, this was the ruling party in Iraq.

Chapter Three

Flight to Turkey

Everything seemed chaotic as we ran towards the mountains and to the nearest Turkish border. Everyone around us were running for their lives, as we were. People drove their cars until they ran out of fuel, and then they ran again. They would drop their luggage when it got too heavy and was preventing them from running as fast as they could. It was like an awesome force, this fear of death, and it seemed to loom over us like a dark shadow. We felt we would never be safe until we reached Turkey, which was the closest country to us. But even then, we ran and we didn't know what was going to happen. Who wanted us? Where were we going to go? It is very hard to capture this feeling of not knowing if you will live or die by the next day. To an average American, it seems so foreign, this fear, but it was so real for me as a child, having to experience this chaotic moment.

It was January, I think, and the weather was very bad. It was cold and rainy, and the whole area around us was rough because we had to go through the mountains. I remember that one of my shoes was completely torn down, and I ended up walking and running with one shoe. I was the youngest in my family, but I had to carry the most things, mainly because I wasn't going to refuse all the things my mother wanted me to carry. However, in Kurdish culture, the youngest person in the family typically does the most things. We brought what we could and everyone carried whatever they could. My bags continuously got heavier because I was carrying flour and the constant rain kept seeping through, making the trip harder and heavier as we went on. The trip to the border took a couple days, but it all seems like a blur, like images here and thoughts there, and it went this way the whole time.

There was a moment while we were running when we had to leave food and other items behind in order to continue running. But, much later, we ran out of food, so all the men would have to go back and try to carry the food they had left back in order for us to continue our journey and not die along the way. When they left, everyone would worry that the Iraqi had gotten to the food already and possibly destroyed it. Then we worried that the men would appear and they would get shot, and we would have to stay where we were and starve to death. This was the fear, but this never happened.

I remember vividly our running. Because there were so many of us running, and everyone was running for their lives, it was very common to get lost, like a child to lose his mother, or mother to lose her children, or for people to lose their families in the vast crowd of people who were running. I remember that there was a woman who was very sick and old, and she got lost from her family. So she stayed with us while we fled. However, she passed away, and we had to bury her in the mountains. I did not know this woman at all, but her death had a profound effect on me.

We finally reached the Turkish border. There were guards there, and they stopped us almost immediately. They wouldn't allow us in at first. Most Turks, Iraqi, and Syrians don't like Kurds. I am not sure what I thought then. It was like everyone hated us, and nobody was going to help us out. We were going to die surrounded by people and countries who would have been more than happy to see us dead. I thought that the soldiers would stop us, notify the Iraqi people that we were at their border, and turn the other way while we all get slaughtered in the middle of the night. These were just assumptions, but we were really afraid and I suppose we thought that anything could happen.

I am not really sure what occurred, but Turkey finally allowed us into their territory. I am sure that there were a lot of talks that happened while we anxiously waited for the Turks to let us in. I am somewhat sure the United States and Europe convinced Turkey to take us in, but I am not really sure. All I know is that when they said we could go into Turkey, I was very relieved. I was going to be safe, and we were not going to die.

Of course, the Kurds were coming from everywhere. They were not just from my hometown. And the Turkish border was very large, so we came from all directions. We didn't all come to one location, of course. There were many checkpoints that we went through. The Turks had built us camps in each of the areas, and it was in one of these camps that my family and I were let into. In the camps, there were many different groups of people from many different organizations and countries, like the United States, United Nations, European Union, and Red Cross. They came in to help us, for clearly our flight to Turkey was something that the world heard a lot about through a lot of headlines.

In this type of situation, we became outcasts. I knew it when I saw my stepmother get pushed by one of the guards. My stepmother had a parcel in her hand when a guard came up to her and, I presume, started arguing. In the end, she must have gotten shoved because people do not fall for no reason, especially her. So, she fell, and there was a small hill that she fell into. We had to go down and help pick her up. She was an older woman and she was bruised all over. The guards had no respect for us and our dignity, our culture, or our safety. Having this feeling of being nothing was terrible.

Of course, there were many instances that occurred on that trip, thousands and thousands. So many that I have lost track of them. People lost their families and died along the way. We lost my mother for a couple days, and that was a scary time. We lost her on the trip, but thankfully we found her again with a family. But, the horrors were unimaginable. The worst was the feeling of complete loss, the utter despair and fear that we would all get killed. The thousands of people running to somewhere, all wiped away, maybe by chemical weapons, or maybe by gunfire. It would be a slaughter and the all the hills and mountains would be filled with dead bodies and corpses everywhere. Such was our fear, and it was great. Until in this situation, no one will know how it feels to be this way. It was as if the whole mountain would bury us, and we would become nobody. Just dust in the ground.

When I look today in the news and see Syrians fleeing their own country, I feel very bad for them, for I was in their situation. I know what desperation feels like. I know how scared they must be to get on a tiny boat and try to sail a vast sea in hope that someone-anyone-would save them from the death that awaits them when they turned around. Those people fleeing have families and friends who die and suffer along the way. They just want to be safe with their families and friends. They don't want to die. They don't want to leave their homes, their cultures, all they know. They leave because they have to, because they are so scared that they must go somewhere. This is what it means to flee your own country.

The camp we stayed was named Mergah. There, we were given basic supplies and got helped by organizations. The camp was terrible, but it was much better than dying, for sure. It was here that some French medical people saw that I knew English well enough that I could converse and be useful. So, I helped them to move things around, to translate for them. Basically, whatever they wanted to do, I did. It gave me a new opportunity to do more things, be productive, and have some kind of purpose while we waited 2 or 3 months in the camp.

Around this time, NATO finally established a No-Fly-Zone around the Kurdish area where had lived. When everything settled down and got calm enough, we went into buses and were sent back to our villages and towns. My family went back to Darkar. Of course, we weren't just dumped there. Many foreign people came with us to help us get a new life and start all over again-to reconstruct. When went to Darkr, everything was completely destroyed. At least the most basic things. There were still people there, it's just that our things were gone and destroyed.

When we were told that we were going back, we got instantly afraid. We did not know if we were going to be threatened again. The officials would have to convince us that we were going to be safe, that we weren't going to get attacked as before. Of course, at first it was hard to comprehend how some organizations could prevent a government regime from enacting a deadly force upon us. We were understandably fearful of the possible outcome. It's a weird feeling, not knowing what could possibly happen once we went back. However, it wasn't like we had much of a choice. We had to go, and so we went back home.

When I finally got to Darkar, and a couple weeks after we had settled in our destroyed home, I heard that the same French organization that I worked with in Mergah was operating nearby in Zakho. So, I went and tried to work with them again. They hired me, and through that organization, I was able to start a run of events that would eventually see my destiny turn out for the better.

It's amazing how a person can be in the most trying of times, and the best moments come along. The past year was spent literally afraid for my life, and suddenly, here I was able to communicate with people that appreciated me and my talent. It made me feel proud to be able to assist these foreign people in my homeland. Being able to assist people and make them happy has always been something that I have enjoyed. As such, I went above and beyond to help people out and do whatever they needed. I saw that this made me really happy, making others happy.

When I did good deeds and helped those needing assistance, more doors opened for me. I was able to meet many new people and be somewhat important to these foreigners. I developed a relationship with many of them and knew that they trusted me for my help. I really respected this, for I always wanted to be known for my generosity and to be respected wherever I went. I may have gotten this from my father, but I tend to view this trait as quite cultural. Many Kurds are generous, going above and beyond to assist others. We respect people who are generous and kind to others. Everyone, I believe, wants to be like this, and I was no different. Everyone in my family is generous and good willing to others.

So, this really helped me as I got to know the French workers in Kurdistan. By helping them, I was able to get respect and trust, and I had the opportunity to be introduced to new things. Eventually, as time went on, these new introductions would eventually open up so many opportunities for me. So, I can't complain that my life was terrible, for I was very much enriched with new things that many people in Kurdistan never have a chance to experience. In that, I am really blessed. And, as the saying goes, good things happen to those who do good things. Or something like that.

Note:

* All images were taken from Kyle Orton and Anneliese Hollmann, portraying the Kurdish flight to Turkey

Chapter Four

Back in Darkar

When we returned, we had to start over. Everything we had or had worked for was gone. Here we were, back in our foreign land. I mean, this was just part of our lives, having to escape and flee, only to come back down and start over. It isn't something we want to do, but it is certainly something that we adapted to doing.

A few weeks in, we found that some Arab family members, whom used to be friends of ours before we left, had stolen almost all the goods that we had left behind and had hidden them under their house. Before, when we used to live there, this family was very quiet and very nice. They seemed like good people because we would see them pray all the time, and treat us very nicely whenever we encountered them. We didn't suspect anything suspicious. So, all of us were extremely mad about our homes being raided and stolen our things when we left. Clearly, it didn't matter that we had developed a relationship with them, they were still going to be selfish. Actually, we found out later that they had been spies for the Iraqi government regime.

Many of the people who had come to help us at the Turkish camps came to help us out in Darkr. This is mainly how we survived, having these organizations help us. Everyone went back to rebuilding the town, and everyone did what they could to start making a little money. My mother started growing a small tomato and cucumber garden, while others found jobs in the nearby city. It was really difficult for us since we lost all of our money when we fled to Turkey, we had to start from almost zero. I continued to work for the French people who I had come to work with in the previous camp, and this enabled me better opportunities to learn better English and encounter more people, something that I had always loved to do. I did practically everything I had done in camp. I translated, I was a tour guide, and I went shopping for the French people, who were doctors. Anything they needed done, I did. However, all this was rather short lived. The French doctors left several months later, and I resumed work elsewhere. However, many companies came and went, providing help for us, and this lasted until 1996.

I later worked for an organization called ACCORN. They were missionaries, and I was doing practically the same job that I had done for the French doctors. It was here that I met a man named Patrick Moy, who would prove pivotal to my life. Patrick Moy was a helping man, who went about practically being a missionary, addressing villagers about how to be safe, building things, and basically being a really good guy. He married a Kurdish woman, so he very much had a love of our culture and people. He was invaluable to me and I owe him a great debt for enabling me to come to the United States when I did. It was through him that I was able to get a job with Global Partners through means of his connection. This company was responsible for building wells for villagers who had no water. I was a body guard for this company. This company was really nice to me because I was in school in Zakho until 1996. When I graduated, they gave me a stationary job working at night by their nearby hospital clinic. It was kind of a struggle because I was going to school and trying to work to make money. I was making about $50 a month, which is almost $80 in today's money. My family really needed the money and it was really good for us. It was really nice of Global Partners because they paid me and allowed me to work so that I could support my family. It was also at this time when my stepsister Shereen, died in a seizure in the well in Orman.

Around this time in Darkar, tensions broke very furiously. A war broke out between the Kurds with Iraq and Turkey. This war saw many people die, and, once again, Darkr was being attacked from the mountains. This type of fighting became almost common place for me. I was certainly aware of the dangers, and saw it as part of daily life. It had a profound effect on me, because it constantly made me anxious that I would die at any moment. It made me aware that death was very near no matter what I did. This was very clear because Darkr got attacked and several people had died in a house by explosives. I remember this day very clearly. Darkr was like no-man's-land, situated between two really hostile parties who hated each other. We were on high alert for many months, fearing for our lives.

Once, when I was walking to the city to work, I turned left on a block, and a rocket suddenly flew past me, where it hit the ground. It happened so quickly, and it could have been over that instant. But, the rocket didn't explode. It appeared that it was one of those old Russian rockets who were internally dead, but I risked no chance. I quickly turned around and started running back home. No sooner was I near my home when another rocket came out of nowhere and practically swept me off my feet with a force that nearly quenched all breath from my lungs. It flew past me in what was probably a lucky instant that I would never experience again. It hit the curb of a house, and seemingly lay there dead like the previous rocket. It was clearly another amazing clearance any other person would have instantly been dead, but again I was lucky. Inside my house, before I even was able to close the door, another rocket came into the yard, fragments flying everywhere, shattering the windows with a powerful wind and sweeping me to the ground with such force that I will never forget that feeling of utter horror of being so close to death. I was never safe, and my life could have ended any of those three times.

However, miraculously, I did not die. The rocket did not explode. It, too, was a dead bomb, and so I was saved thrice. But, each time I was fearful, and the fear grew worse. I suddenly realized that I did not want to be there, that I could not be safe there. I was in constant fear everywhere, unsure whenever I stepped out the door that I would come back alive. This was not a life I really aspired to. Everyone in the village came to our house that day, believing that we had all died. I would look at myself, almost in amazement, looking and touching my hands to see if I was real, and how on earth I survived three blasts. I couldn't believe it. It was like a slow motion movie.

Meanwhile, while all this was happening to my town, Saddam Hussein had given amnesty to all Kurds. There was, however, an exception. He did not give amnesty to those Kurds who had helped the Westerns, meaning Americans or Europeans. Unfortunately, this was well against me, for I had volunteered and helped plenty of Westerns, including working for them. I wasn't sure what to do. I felt threatened and afraid that they were going after me. My family was in trouble, and most especially me, for I was actually working for Americans. To be caught helping Americans would have meant me getting hanged. Thus, I had no option. I had to leave and go somewhere safer.

President Bill Clinton of the United States had apparently allowed about 5,000 visas to those Kurds helping American cause in the Iraqi Kurdish war, and as such, because I worked for an American company, I applied for this visa. I was able to get it, and I was told that I could take someone else, since I was single. So, I decided to take my mother with me. My oldest brother, who worked as a bodyguard for Americans in Kurdistan, also came with me and brought his family, since he was married. We would needed each other in the coming years, so it was important that I went with family.

We went to a camp in Turkey called Silopi while awaiting our flight. Thousands of Kurds came to see us off, waving and hoping to see us again. For us, it was unbelievable that we would be leaving our homeland to escape possible death. I was not sure if I would ever see my family again. However, I was excited, too, because I was going to America. People say this experience is amazing, and it is. America is amazing. I had hopes for anything to happen. It was as if opportunities were everywhere, and I could make anything of myself. I was very thankful that America would take me and my immediate family. I don't think I would have lived to see a family of my own if I had not left. When I got on that plane in Batman, Turkey, and headed off, I felt as if the planed tugged me a bit, wanting me not to leave. Of course, it was all gravity, but I had never been on a plane before, so it was a new experience. In several minutes, it was as the pull left me and I was suddenly released. Here again, to start over, in the United

States of America. As I looked out the window, I felt relieved. It was going to be good.

A very ironic situation had occurred in Kurdistan that is quite interesting, and it is quite important to the story of my life. In about 1993 or so, in the Kurdish mountains, a British plane crashed. This incident could have gone completely wrong. After all, the pilot was injured, but he could have been captured and a whole series of bad events could have escalated from there. However, the pilot was found by Hayran Saleh and his men and they stood there for a 15 days protecting the pilot as they awaited for his rescue. He ensured that the pilot was taken care of, and when this British pilot had been rescued, Hayran Saleh received a certificate, a big award, for his act of heroism. Almost instantly, this man became famous throughout Kurdistan, although he certainly was before that incident anyway for fighting against the Saddam regime. But, he became more famous for his charity and acts of kindness. When I heard this story, I was truly amazed. I really respected this man. I knew little about him, but he was someone I probably would have wanted to sit down with and knew he would be a great man. I mean, this man was offered to come to America with his family, but he decided to stay in Kurdistan and fight the regime. I never really thought about it too much, honestly. It's ironic, you know, because what appeared as something so distant was really quite close. Several years later, I would marry his daughter.

This is the award that Fatima's father, Hayran Saleh, was given when he and his men protected the British pilot whose plane went down in the mountains.

Chapter Five

America

I had never imagined what type of options or opportunities awaited in the United States. I had heard many stories and I cherished what I knew about this great country, but it felt almost unreal when I landed several hours later at night in the U.S. territory of Guam, an island in the Pacific Ocean. There, I was placed in one of the military camps called Anderson South. My brother was with me, and in another camp, called Tejan, people from my village of Darkr, who were also refugees, were also stationed. I therefore came to know almost everyone and had a good experience while I was there.

I was in Guam from December 1996 to February 1997. As far as experiences go, this was definitely one of the best I had ever had in my life. The island was incredibly beautiful. Beaches were everywhere, and the weather was spectacular. The rain drizzled for what seemed to be an endless time, but actually would stop after a while. The air always smelled fresh and the food was amazing. In our free time, we played football in our local football league. Although I had asked the people from the Tejan Camp, named Zakho, if I could join their team, they turned me down due to my young age. So, I created my own team, GP (Global Partners). We reached the semifinals and played the Tejan Camp. However, due to the game getting so aggressive (and fearing we could get hurt), we forfeited. Needless to say, in the final, the Zakho team never even won because the game was cancelled because a fight broke out.

The camp provided us with educational resources, teaching us how to better speak the English language, and how to go about doing the most basic things, such as writing checks and filling out tax forms. We learned the customs and history of the United States, and we underwent or were subjected to background checks. Everything was provided for us, and we had help in getting our visas and paperwork done. Everyone at the camp was extremely respectful and nice to us, which was something I really enjoyed about Guam. Not only this, but the people there appreciated us and what we had done for America. They left us in peace and gave us mosques to pray in. It was amazing because it seemed as if they understood us, and respected us for who we were. I had no regrets at Guam. I felt very blessed to be in such a good place, and to be helped by really nice people. Meanwhile, my brother and I continued to translate for the military officials. We awaited the location of our soon-to-be-home.

After we had done everything and got what we needed, the government officials went around and asked us where we wanted to go in the States. Usually this is how the procedure went. People usually had connections in the States, so they usually went to the cities where their friends or family members were located. While I was there, the main city most everyone was going to was Dallas, Texas. When they asked me where I wanted to go, I stated Dallas as my choice. However, the officials wanted me to go elsewhere. They asked me if I would consider St. Louis. I told them I had no idea about this city, or where it was located. So, I asked them what the nearest city to St. Louis was. They said Chicago. I knew Chicago. It sounded familiar, and I said that I would go to St. Louis since I knew that Chicago was nearby.

I'm not really sure why Chicago affected me so at that moment. I didn't really want to go into a city where I had nobody and knew no one. I wanted familiarity and it seemed, no matter how weird, that recognizing my image of Chicago, and all its fabrications I had never experienced, was enough to push me to go to St. Louis. I suppose, as a refugee, I was happy wherever I could go and be safe. I just wanted to ensure my family was safe and happy, and any place that offered this I was fine with. I think I was quite nervous of the unknown, so I grasped to the familiarity of the name Chicago, even though I had never been there at that time.

The officials told me that if I went to St. Louis, stayed there for a little while, and then not like it, I could go wherever I liked. I thought this was a pretty good plan, so I decided that St. Louis was the place to go first. I remember this moment quite clearly, because an emotional event occurred. My mother arrived in San Francisco, the first city in the States. When she arrived, my mother went to the ground and started crying. She said that she wouldn't move-or go anywhere-until she knew where my brother's family was going to. When I arrived, some workers at the airport took us to the immigration office, where they treated us very respectfully and showed real kindness. They told us everything we needed to know in great detail, outlining the exact apartment where we were to be stationed in St. Louis, and how we were to get there. They told us that my brother's family would be joining in St. Louis in a couple of weeks, as well. They answered all of our questions patiently until we had no more concerns. It was incredible, like a huge weight of uncertainty was lifted from our shoulders. It was like we suddenly knew exactly what was going to happen, and that we were going to be okay. My mother was extremely relieved and happy, and we proceeded on to St. Louis at ease.

We went to a place called Minnesota Street in East St. Louis. It was a rough neighborhood, but we made do with the two apartments that we had. I was accustomed to shootings almost daily, but we only had to be there for only a year. Almost immediately after coming to St. Louis, my brother, who came a few weeks after me, and I went out and got jobs. We also attended the International Institute to learn better English and obtain resources to go out in society and work. There was a Jewish Family Services that helped provide and sponsor everything we needed. They helped us essentially help ourselves, and I am constantly in their debt for helping us. Basically, we worked to save enough money to progress to a better home. I was eager to settle down and have a quiet life, but working towards it was difficult. I was extremely determined, though, and with my brother, we had enough to go northwest of the area, by the Botanical Gardens.

My first job in the first year in the States was at the Adam's Mark Hotel. I did room dining. However, the second year, I got another job in Earth City at Dimac Direct, as a machine operator. I had this job for two years, until 2000. Dimac Direct, however, shut down in 2001, so I was extremely lucky to have had the benefit of working there before this happened. The company was extremely good to me because whenever I did overproduction, I would get a bonus. Thus, I would overproduce, and I almost always got bonuses by continuously working harder and harder every week. My brother worked with me, so it was really nice to be able to make decent money and be able to have someone there to experience that with. Everything was really looking up for me.

After Dimac Direct shut down, my brother and I found a job at Worldhandlers, where I did practically the same thing that I had done previously as a machine operator. I had this job until right after September 11, 2001. My mother was quite ill, so she stayed at home while we took care of her. One of my brothers was able to come to the United States because my mother applied for his visa. Within a year, he was with us, enabling us to have more of us to depend upon. For free time, I used to go play at Towergrove Park. I hadn't lost my skills in football, and I continued to play for about four more years. I even hosted some parties, as well.

Basically, my life had changed dramatically. I learned really quickly the concept of working hard. You ultimately get what you put into your work. Every day I would go to work, and work harder, knowing that the more I worked and put my energy in doing the best I could, the more I was going to progress. That's essentially what was happening to me. I continued to earn more money, better experience, and a respect from my peers and supervisors. As long as I worked, and worked hard, I could do pretty much anything I wanted.

I guess this is the beauty of the United States. When people come over to the states, they see opportunities. They see and appreciate the opportunities available, no matter what they are, and they go for them. For me, I did just that. I worked and worked, and focused on doing my best. Everything was working out for me, and I was really quite content with my life. I was happy to be in a safe area where I could work in peace and just focus on doing what I needed and wanted to do in life. I really couldn't ask for anything better.

When people mention the American dream, I can certainly say that I had it. I was determined to succeed and progress. I had the immigrant desire to work hard and start over. Of course, I still thought about my people back home. Not a day goes back when I don't think about them. However, I'm not really an immigrant. I didn't really want to leave Kurdistan. I left because I had to. I left because I was going to die otherwise. I believe it was the right choice. I hoped I was right.

It was around this time that I decided I wanted to write a book about my life. I'm not sure what drove me to that decision. I know that I thought that I had a pretty interesting story to tell. At the same time, though, I thought about how little people knew about my country. I thought about how many people could not be able come to America and experience my life. I thought about the struggles my people still endure in Kurdistan. The Kurds were surrounded by Syrians, Iraqi, Iranians, and Turks. Nowhere could they turn. It was like they were swallowed whole, distant in their own land, tiny voices that couldn't ever be heard. And the only thing that separated and protected them from the world was the mountains. But, I was beyond those mountains. In fact, I never see them anymore. But, my voice was here, and my people were back home. So, I suppose when I thought about it, I knew I had to let people know my story. I'm only one voice, but there are many voices over the mountains. So, I knew I had to write my life story because my life was their lives, and my voice was their voices.

Thus, after several years, my life took a different turn. Because soon I was to meet my wife and get married and have kids and do the typical things that a father must do. Of course, for that to occur, I had to go back home for a while, to see my family that I had left behind and to reminisce about the days when I was a child back in Darkr. Those days were far gone, but memories live on forever. So, there I was, on a plane again, going back to the mountains of the Middle East. Back home, in Kurdistan.

Chapter Six

Fatima

A majority of my life was spent thinking about what I myself went through and how I felt about things. However, a major part of my life was the moment I got married to my wife, Fatima. The process to get her over to the U.S. was a very long one. It took several years, and a lot of paperwork. The incidents of September 11th, 2001 halted the paperwork for a few years, and in that time, it was really quite difficult for me to get anything going.

At the time that I had departed to Kurdistan, I was still working for Worldhandlers with my younger brother. My older brother worked for Ambassador St. Louis Parking, and we were all doing relatively well. So, you know, I felt very comfortable going back home to see my family and home town. There were some things that had occurred, and it just seemed like a prime time to go back. My stepmother had passed away and I wanted to go and show my respects. I wanted to see how my other family members were doing and to see to the properties that I still had in in my name back in Kurdistan.

I was at my sister's house. She was talking about a particular woman in the village of Orman, whom she wanted for me to meet. She thought that perhaps I should just go and see whether I liked this woman. It was a setting up. I was getting older and I was at the age of marriage, and in Kurdistan, it was customary for men to be introduced to women for a possible marriage. I didn't think too much about it, really. I agreed to go because I didn't see any reason to decline the offer. So, we went to Ranya to visit this particular woman's family, because my mother knew her mother. It went this way until we showed up at the house and had a meal with the family.

Before I married, I went to my hometown to Orman. I am on the main street, in the typical Kurdish clothes.

This is when I met Fatima. It is hard to describe the feeling I had then when I first saw her. I instantly liked her. She was extremely pretty, with dark black hair and dark eyes with long eyelashes. She was like one of those gorgeous girls that you read about in the *One Thousand and One Nights*. She was like poetry to the eyes. There are no words for her. She just was. The moment I stepped into the home, I knew that she was a keeper, and I felt I had to walk away with her saying that she wanted to marry me. I knew that she was the one for me, so I went to my mother and said that I wanted to marry her. I asked her father, Hayran Saleh, who was the man whom I had heard so many famous stories about (especially the one about saving the British pilot), whether he would allow her hand in marriage. He said that he was in agreement, as long as Fatima agreed. Fatima was silent at first, but then she laughed, so knew that she agreed to marry me.

There was a funny scenario that occurred between Fatima and me. Because I was so incredibly shy, I just sat in the room while everyone walked out from the living room. Suddenly, however, I heard someone lock the door. So, I started yelling, wondering if someone was setting me up for something bad to happen. However, Fatima came around the window and saw me locked in the room. She came back, with a red face and shyly apologized to me. It was funny, you see, because it was a special moment. Til this day, I think she did this on purpose. Perhaps she liked me too. I don't know. Perhaps her beautiful black eyes wouldn't admit it then or now, but I have a good inclination. After all, at the time, I wasn't getting bald. I was a handsome man.

The preparations and paperwork began, according to the culture. The small parties began to get everything done, and we got married in a small ceremony a few months later. According to the culture, should the marriage not work out, I would offer the family 30 grams of gold, which would be equivalent to about $1,300 in today's money. In our culture, this was done to prevent us husbands from leaving the wife. However, we were not worried in such matters. I was sure that I we would work things out. I just needed to apply for her visa, and bring her with me to the United States.

My wedding photo. We got married in Duhok, Iraq. Notice that at the time I had great hair. It's one trait of mine I truly miss nowadays.

I went back home and started applying for my wife's visa right away. However, at the time, this was difficult. I was a permanent resident and so this was going to be quite difficult to do given my status in the States. Thus, I did all the paperwork in that status, while I awaited the situation hopefully to look in my favor. No sooner had I turned in the paperwork when the attacks on the twin towers in New York occurred. This caused me to get especially nervous, because I was a Muslim from the Middle East and because all my effort in trying to get Fatima to come to the States was instantly halted. It was absolutely horrible given the circumstances, and I was actually scared that perhaps other people might turn on me and see me as part of the incident that had occurred. I suppose that when a person observes such events, then they view it from an outside perspective. However, given that the people who did this act were from the Middle East, the concept of terror was really strong and many people suddenly seemed to define us by these incidents. Of course, very few of us are this violent and portray this much hate, so I was quite shocked that suddenly this view grew much stronger after 9/11. Given the rise of the hate crimes towards Muslims, I thought that perhaps I too would get targeted.

Having my wife's visa paperwork terminated was a real blow to me. I didn't know what to do. How was I going to reconcile with my wife? Would we always live apart? Would I have to go back home in order to live with her and raise a family? I wasn't sure, but I still maintained communication with her via Skype and phone. I tried to continue my life the best way I could, in the best way possible. I got rather bored with my job as a machine operator. Also, given that my job was rather far away, I decided to go work with my older brother Sabah at Ambassador Valet Parking. I did this from 2001 to 2006. Meanwhile, I went to college at Forest Park Community College, where I got an Associate's in Criminal Justice. I had a plan to continue my education, but I put it off for a bit while I figured out what I was going to do with my life. I seemingly was going through some kind of mental crisis in trying to figure out what to do, but I was trying to fill my time with something productive.

I finally moved to a new house in Thozlan Avenue, in a much nicer neighborhood, and a much bigger house. It had to be a big house because everyone in my family- my mother and brothers and their family- were in this house. However, I was not really satisfied. Given that things weren't looking too well for me when it came to the visa process, I decided to go back home and live with Fatima. I had a hope that I could just take the risk and live with Fatima in Dohuk. So, I left in October of 2004, for Kurdistan, to meet my wife.

While there, I celebrated with all my family in being able to see my wife again. It was a huge party, close to almost 400 people, so it was clear to me that my coming back could be beneficial for me. I stayed at my sister's house for about two months. While there, my family back home had received a letter from the Immigration Office asking me where I wanted to do an interview at an American Embassy for my wife's visa acceptance. They had allocated me two options-either Turkey or Jordan.

Suddenly, hope rushed back into me, and I quickly came back to the States to get everything ready. Suddenly, everything looked up and I was happy and dancing inside, singing Kurdish songs in my heart because now I had a chance to bring my wife with me to America. While here in the U.S., I continued to work. I decided that I would go to the American Embassy in Amman, Jordan to get the interview done. The Immigration Office agreed that I could go to Jordan for the interview, but did not give me a date and time for this to occur. So, I contacted a lawyer in Amman to help me speed up my case. However, while I was waiting for my lawyer to get back with me for the date of the interview at the Embassy, I suddenly received another letter stating that I could take the citizenship test. I was extremely happy because I was definitely knew that I would pass it, and once I passed it, it would take about a month before I would go and obtain my ceremonial certificate of citizenship.

In May of 2005, I obtained my citizenship, and I immediately drove to Chicago to get my passport that same day. Given that my status changed from Permanent Resident to citizen, I knew my case changed, and there would be a much quicker process once I got to Amman. So, I purchased my ticket within a few days and flew out to Amman, Jordan, to meet my lawyer personally. I gave her a copy of my citizenship ecstatically, because suddenly everything was going to be much easier for me and my wife. Things were looking up, and it was amazing.

From Amman, I drove to Damascus, Syria, and from there I drove to the border between Iraq and Syria. My brother had driven my wife to the border, so I met Fatima there and we both drove back to Amman. We spent seven months in Amman, waiting. We had a date for the interview and everything, but we were stalled several times. The American Embassy had a lot of interviews to do because there were more than just myself and my wife hoping to come back to the States. There were a lot of Kurds trying to get their families to come. So, we had to wait. While waiting, I translated for other peoples and their families while they had their interviews. However, suddenly, for no reason at all, the process got held up. Suddenly, families could not just translate for others when interviewing. This was a critical problem for me because my wife did not know any English so I knew I had to be her personal translator for her interview. Now, however, the Embassy would only allow their own personnel translators to do the interviews. This would have been ok with us, but to get a translator for my wife would be extremely difficult because the Embassy translators were extremely booked. If we waited to make an appointment with one of them, it would take many months. It was another obstacle in our way, one certainly that made me quite irritated and impatient.

However, as luck should have it, our lawyer came back and told us that Fatima could take the interview and avoid waiting if she could speak Arabic, English, Turkish, and Persian. Fatima clearly spoke no English, so that was out of the question. Her Arabic was okay, but she wasn't confident with this language given the dialects. Her Turkish was excellent, but Persian was her language because this was the language she knew the best, and she chose to take the interview in that language.

At five a.m. in the morning for the eight o'clock interview, we waited outside of the Embassy. We shuffled in nervously as I took my seat and waited for Fatima's name to be called. When they called my wife, I tried walking with her to the interview, but I was told to wait back at the lobby. So, I did. For what seemed like eternity, I stared at the many people bustling in the Embassy with my heart racing, wondering how wrong everything could go, but hoping that everything was going to be okay. I was praying and hoping so much. I had sweat on my forehead while I anticipated the outcome.

After Fatima came out the clear doors, they asked for her Iraqi passport. To us, this seemed quite strange because, you know, your passport is your life when you're an immigrant or a refugee. It's what defines us and what gets us in places. Wherever and whenever we go anywhere, this is the document people demand they see from us, and now that they took my wife's passport, it seemed that her identity-her existence, rather-was taken away. This was a curious thing, and when we got back to our apartment, we called our lawyer to ask her what this meant. However, she seemed rather optimistic about the situation, stating that this was a good sign of things to come, and would probably just mean that her interview went alright.

Two days later, we got a call from our lawyer, stating that we needed to go back to the Embassy to get Fatima's passport, stamped with an American visa. Wow. What a day for us. It was so unreal for us. Almost a year in the Middle East and all the trials, ups and downs, and now we were staring at a stamp on a piece of paper. A stamp. That's all it was. All the worries and constant upsets. It seemed so simple. But, there we were. We finally did it. A year in the making. What a relief!

Soon afterwards, we bought our tickets to fly home. At the airport in Chicago, the Immigration Office handed my wife an equivalence of a green card that was good for 10 years. Everything then proceeded as normal, me being much happier and having more purpose in life. We lived in the same big house with my family on Thozlan Avenue for the next two years. I had my first child, Aland, there. My wife worked at Assex, which was a sowing company that made airbags for airplanes. I started working as a valet and security at Plaza in Clayton in 2006. I had this job until 2010, when another great opportunity arose that would change my life and my chances for an even better future. Meanwhile, in 2008, Fatima and I decided to move to our current home in Affton.

I guess that throughout this time, I realized even more the effect that the American dream had on me. I constantly worked hard, and I eventually got what I dreamed for. Nobody had told me it was going to be easy, nor did I expect it. In America, everything was possible. There was a need to be patient and work through processes, but everything only got better for me. I met a lot of really nice people along the way, which I must be thankful for. My lawyer in Amman was amazing. My family assisting me in all my difficulties were amazing. The people in the American Embassy, at the Chicago airport, everyone that smiled at me and made me laugh- they all helped me along the way. It's amazing how something so simple could be so helpful. I may not have been an immigrant on a boat going to Ellis Island, seeing the Statue of Liberty raise her arm in the sky with a golden light that seemed to shine from halfway across the world. It looked so inviting and protective. However, seeing my wife's visa stamped on her passport seemed to give me the same message. It seemed to say *"Give me your tired, your poor, Your huddled masses yearning to breathe free, The wretched refuse of your teeming shore. Send these, the homeless, tempest-tossed to me, I lift my lamp beside the golden door."* What a land America was, to be what my home couldn't be. And now, here I was, with my wife, in a wonderful land of opportunities.

Chapter Seven

Best Job in the World

In 2010, a friend of mine from Nashville was going to Virginia to hopefully get a job for the Department of Defense as a linguist with the Global Linguist Solution, which contracts with the US military. He told me about it, and convinced me that I should apply as well. So, I called the Department, and applied. The people on the line told me to await a phone exam, which I promptly took. The people told me to come to Virginia to get a more thorough examination of my background as my next step in the process. I thought about it, and kind of self-reflected about this whole thing.

It hit me, this philosophical thought. I sincerely wanted to promote myself, to find new opportunities, and do something new. At the same time, though, I thought about how America had helped me out. Contrary to the popular opinion, this country had done a lot for me. I felt I was in debt to its sincerity in helping me achieve my dreams and ambitions. Thus, I felt that going into the military and serving as a linguist was going to really help and give back for all that the US had done for me. I wasn't hoping to get recognized or anything. I kind of felt it was my duty. So, I went to Virginia promptly, not thinking twice about the decision.

In Virginia, I went through the one week process, where we had to do a medical, physical, written, and oral exams. Meanwhile, my background was once again looked into extensively. I passed this week, and headed off to Georgia where we had another rigorous week of what we expected to encounter in Iraq. Basically, it was the training meant for military people, but it was the first week of training when I was really going to be serving the military. After the two weeks of training, we headed off to Kuwait, to an American military base.

In official military gear, ready to meet with Iraqi officials. I personally translated for the Commander of 6-8 Cav.

Kuwait was hot. We lived in the desert, in tents, by the border of Iraq. After a few days, we were given an assignment at the biggest American air force base in Balad, Iraq. I stayed there about a few months, translating for the American officers. Afterwards, I went to the headquarters in Bagdad, Iraq, while I waited for new assignments. The main job that I did extensively was in Talafer, Mosul, Iraq, where I could interact with Kurds and Arabs, since I was well accustomed to their culture and their language. After six months of working there, I was stationed to work alongside the Commander of the base in traveling outside the base in her expeditions. I worked hard and diligently there, and I enjoyed my time being helpful. It was definitely a good opportunity because the Commander preferred me. I was bilingual, being able to speak Arabic and Kurd, which was ideal for the base because they did not have to get individual interpreters for each of the languages. I worked at the base until the whole Iraqi operation was over, in 2011, when President Obama ordered the completion of the withdrawal of troops in Iraq.

Picture in front of the usual lineup and briefing that was customary whenever a group of soldiers left the base.

That particular day, when we had to depart, we were ready to leave by 20:00 military time. I sat with the Commander in his Humvee, and we drove away slowly, nonstop, in the middle of the night, always alert. It was a very scary, because we didn't really know what could happen. We were on high alert, ready for a possible assault. For this reason, we had gunners on the lookout. We drove to the Kuwait border, but we encountered a huge desert storm along the way. We had to stop for a few hours because we were not able to see anything. We ended up calling the nearest base for air support to ensure for our safety. This was extremely scary for me because the danger was truly real. Anybody could have attacked us.

A typical desert storm in southern Iraq. In this picture, this is our base in the middle of a storm. In these situations, you couldn't see anything. All operations halted until the storm was done, which usually lasted several hours.

Needless to say, we were fine, but it was a day for me to remember. Back in Kuwait, we gathered all our gear and headed back home. I was offered a job to stay in Kuwait and continue to work for the US military, but I decided to go back home to my family. Back in the States, I was also offered a job in August 2012 to work for the State Department in the Kurdish capital of Irbil, Iraq in the American Consulate. I asked Global Linguist Solutions to wait a little bit, because my wife was due with our third child, Lara, and I wanted to be there for her. I was told that they would hold the position for me; however, if someone qualified could take the position, they would offer them that job. My best friend from Nashville took that position, but I don't regret my choice.

The military was a really good experience for me. I know that many people in the United States are greatly in disagreement about the U.S. intervening in Iraq and taking out Saddam Hussein. However, I am from that region, and I actually worked there. I encountered the presence of American troops and their ambition and caring actions in helping the Iraqi people rebuild their homes and have better lives. I have so much respect in how much effort the troops placed in doing what they believed was the good for the community. Not to mention the fact that the awful dictator, Saddam Hussein, was finally ousted. The man who killed so many people using chemical weapons and who murdered my own people. He was finally gone. I definitely agree that the situation after his death was a difficult adjustment; however, I have seen the sincere effort the American troops had in trying to give their best. They lost their lives and had to experience a difficult task in trying to rebuild a country completely in chaos. I know that, back home, it's very easy to criticize what troops do so far away from home. Being so far away makes it very easy to judge actions by other people, especially when details are left out and when experiences are not felt. I think that there should be more respect for these people who dedicate their lives to helping America achieve its goals and dreams abroad. We never truly know the effect of our actions, but we should definitely respect the fact that we tried our best to do what we believed was right, even if it might not have been.

To be able to experience those moments with the military was extremely special for me. Richard Johnson, Command Sergeant Major of my unit, wrote a really special recommendation letter about me where he stated that my "communication skills in both Kurdish and Arabic were a great asset to this command and the accomplishment of our mission", words that really mean a lot to me because it meant that I was a critical member of what was occurring at the base. Christopher Conner, Captain of my unit, also said that he "would trust" me to be a member of his Personal Security Detachment unit. In one situation, he states, "When I was asking for his help he was able to diffuse a very deadly situation between a Kurdish faction and the Arabic Military leaders". I remember this situation vividly and I am proud of preventing what could have been a really terrible outcome. These types of compliments made me feel very happy that I was part of something bigger and for the benefit of the United States. I felt I had done my duty, and when President Obama sent us home, I felt that I had accomplished what I had sent myself out to do.

Squatting on top of Saddam Hussein's palace in Bagdad, Iraq. It was a proud moment for me because the man who was responsible for the many deaths of my people was finally gone.

I went back home and was out of work for a few months. However, I found a wonderful job working for the Ritz Carlton through a job opening notification from a friend. I was a bellman, helping guests with their luggage and showing them their rooms. I got great pay, and I settled down in a routine lifestyle, having accomplished what I believe is my American dream. Time went on and I carried on. I even went back to visit Kurdistan in 2012, arriving in Dohuk in what happened to be the biggest snowfall they had received in twenty years. While there, I encountered people who seemed to have gotten more knowledge and seemed more educated than what had been in the past. I thought about it, and I decided I would go back to school and obtain my Bachelor's Degree in Criminal Justice. I had wanted to do this all along, and realizing that I could do something different in the future in an area I sincerely loved, I enrolled at the University of Missouri-St. Louis.

This is essentially how this whole process of this book came to life. In the small moments that exist, special things happen at just the right times. In the summer of 2014, I enrolled in a summer class to get some credits out of the way. I wanted to take an easy-to-get-out-of-the-way course, so I chose an anthropology class called "Cultural Traditions". It was a pretty easy class, not one that required much studying. However, on a certain day, I came to class a few minutes before it started and was watching Brazil play a team in the World Cup on my phone. It was just a regular day, and I noticed a young kid who was sitting in the back, watching another game that was being played that day in the World Cup. I looked at him and his candid attitude. He had a football jersey on and his legs sprawled on the nearby chairs. He clearly looked bored and anyone could tell that he didn't want to be here. It humored me, seeing this kid. So, I looked back and got his attention.

"Hey, I've seen you before", I said. "What's your name?"

The lad looked up and turned his shoulder to show a printed name on the back of his Tottenham Hotspurs Jersey. It said "BURCEA" in bold black letters.

"But you can just call me Nicolae", he said.

Afterword

Nicolae Burcea and I would become good friends by the end of that summer. He would continue to be really good friends with me even after we took the Cultural Traditions class. Nicolae had a knack for writing, which was really a struggle for me. We would work together on my homework. I would bring him to my house for lunch while we discussed the history of my country. He was really quite a curious fellow because he enjoyed learning about practically everything. He seemed to have a good understanding of culture and history because he was studying International Relations, specifically focused on the Middle East and the Balkan areas. It also helped that he was born in Romania and had traveled and read quite extensively about what I had lived through and done in my life.

After relating my story to Nicolae, it became clear that, for all the people I met in my life, he was the one that I most comfortable knowing he would do a great job in helping me write my book. He loved to write, and his being eager to know about my life and my people meant he actually cared to understand what Kurdistan was like. He also was a traveler, so he did have an exclusive understanding about how life events affected people. It was for this reason that I brought up writing my book to him.

Now, Nicolae's writing abilities are quite unusual. I have never seen a person in my life who can do what he does with words. Starting off, Nicolae is a charismatic fellow, funny and always curious. Like me, he loves football and constantly plays it. His knowledge about world affairs is extensive, and he is very social and outgoing. While in college, he was involved in various organizations, took an almost unbelievable load of 24 plus credit hours per semester, and he worked and volunteered around the school. His ability to navigate all these events was amazing, but these things weren't the most remarkable things about him.

The most remarkable thing with Nicolae is his ability to procrastinate. While I sat busily writing notes in class, he was always on his computer watching football games or reading articles on foreign affairs. He never took any notes, and all his notebooks in his book bag remained clean and empty for the two years that he was in the university. Whereas I studied hard for the tests in my classes, Nicolae never studied for any of his classes. Most of the time, he never even read the materials that the professors instructed us to read. No. Nicolae would come in, take the tests, and magically breeze through. He was just one of those people who didn't have to do anything. He could just do what a million of us students would struggle to achieve. This kid always managed to get practically perfect scores on anything he tried. Nicolae became quite famous in the University for being able to write whole essays in a matter of a few hours, almost the night before or the hours right before class. I have seen this incredible ability first hand when he typed a difficult 10 page paper in a brisk hour and forty five minutes. It was quite amazing, you see, because that paper would end up being one of the best in whatever class he was writing it for, and he would walk away with an almost perfect score without having broken a sweat. A person with this ability is quite amazing, and I've always pondered about Nicolae. If he worked so well under pressure and wrote so well in two hours, I wonder how much better his papers would be if he actually dedicated weeks to them, like most of us college students. I never would know, honestly, because if there was one thing that was consistent about Nicolae, it was that he was going to procrastinate on anything that allowed him time to do other things.

I asked Nicolae to help me write my book two years ago, in the summer of 2014. After listening to my story, he went back to his dorm and quickly wrote the whole story in a matter of five hours. I never really got to read the text because he had submitted it to an editor for final revisions. That story was in third person, and it was clear that many things had gone wrong. For one, Nicolae could not remember everything that I had told him exactly, word for word. Secondly, he realized he couldn't really expand on anything about Kurdistan because he had never lived my life nor seen what I had seen. He told me he felt like the book was also rather dull because it seemed very "detached".

He decided to simply help me write notes for him the best way I could, and just type down what I said and wrote in the most grammatically correct way possible. We spoke to each other on every paragraph and tried to come up with the best way of writing the description of my life. It was clear to Nicolae that I wanted an authentic voice, and he was very careful in always asking me if the sentences made sense to me and if I understood them the same way that I lived them. We worked so closely on the text that I believe he is the only person in my life that knows most about me other than myself. I shared with him everything, and this bond developed into a close friendship that I am forever thankful for. Of course, the elaborations of the historical events he knew much about, so he took liberty to expand on those things in the book. But, he tends to push things off, and I would joke with him about it. Until recently.

Nicolae graduated college exactly a year after I did, in May of 2016. He got accepted into a European diplomatic academy around this time, and he was set to leave for Europe in mid-September of 2016. But as the time grew near, he started rewriting the whole book again, this time in first person. It took a much longer time because he had to listen to the recordings, read the notes I had presented to him about my life, rearrange the words I spoke so that they made clear and structural sense, and then write the text in a better way that was relatable to the common reader. We would see each other and go over the texts, making sure I agreed with everything and everything was correct. This partnership was amazing because it was the first time either of us had done anything like this.

While all this was occurring, I had done a lot of things throughout the year. Due to my service and hospitality at work, I became a quick favorite in the Ritz Carlton Hotel. Developing this respect wasn't difficult for me because I have always been hardworking and diligent. However, I really enjoyed this job because of the number of wonderful people I encountered every day. I have accomplished, essentially, my American dream. I am happy and content, I have a beautiful family and a good job, and I'm surrounded by good friends. Every now and then, something is added to make it more extraordinary.

In May 2015, I graduated with a Bachelor's degree in Criminal Justice from the University of Missouri St. Louis. That year, I also received the "Hospitality Superhero of the Year" of the St. Louis region. Besides my usual business that I try to instill with care and professionalism, an incident that had occurred began to get some news attention. A couple and their little girl were guests in our hotel that year and I overheard the young girl say that she liked the robe our hotel provided and that she would love to have one just like it. I did not really think too much about it, but several months later, I heard that the little girl was sick and in the hospital. I tracked the young girl's family and I ordered a robe in her size. I drove to their home and gave the robe to the family, in hope that this would cheer her up and make her feel better. For this, the family was extremely thankful, and they were sure that this really helped her during her first chemotherapy.

The recognition award ceremony pamphlet, when I received my Super Hero of the Year, Hospitality Award for 2015.

The Hospitality Superhero award means so much to me because it tells a lot about my character. I desire to be helpful and to have a truly good impression on people. I want to ensure others are happy, for there is nothing better than a smile on someone's face. It might just be the most beautiful thing in this whole world. Given that I am a Muslim, I do want to showcase small acts of kindness to people, because I believe this is what's right and good in the eyes of Allah. It gives me joy when others are happy and they have what they need. Indeed, it may stem from my father. I have always looked up to him even though he had died when I was very young. I feel I would make him extremely proud had he been alive to see me win this award.

I was rewarded by being given a vacation anywhere that there was a Ritz Carlton, all-expense paid. I decided to take my family to Amelia Island in Florida for five days, and it was very spectacular. Once again, it only reiterated my point that whenever people work hard for things, they get rewarded for the good things they do for others. I couldn't ask for more. I am always and every day thankful for my life and how things have gone for me. There isn't a day that goes by when I don't think about how much I owe the United States and the friends and family who have gotten me to where I am now, where I want to be.

Of course, I also remember that I have an obligation to my home country, as well. I feel that Kurdistan needs to be acknowledged and known to the world. For this reason, I write this book, in hope that somebody can be inspired to know more about it and my people. Perhaps, too, that others might feel that they, too, can accomplish anything if they try as hard as they can.

The world is a very large place, and there are exceptions and forces through which anything can happen. If people believe and try, then anything can occur. We may be voices engulfed by hollow ground and vast enclosures, but we still exist and have an ability to be heard. We are all Voices over the Mountains.

Picture of my family taken at the Ritz Carlton hotel in Amelia Island, Florida.

-

      I drove up to the Saint Louis Lambert Airport and I watched as Nicolae's usual bored and I-can't-wait-for-this-to-be-over attitude flared up on his face. He was back on his phone again, reading articles about what was happening in the world. It seemed he was good about drowning out all the noises, and seemed heavily focused on his study. In his hand he held a new book on the Middle East, recently just bought with the Barnes and Noble gift card I had given him the other day. We decided we were going to meet this coming winter. I will take him to my home in Kurdistan, starting with my birthplace in Orman. The whole story will come alive for him, and he will see and smell everything that I went through. He will taste the food that brings us Kurds together, hear the music that speaks about our passions and home, and see the rolling hills and mountains that keep us shut away from the rest of the world. He doesn't know it, but he will come to understand who we are and where we are going. It's been a long road, but it's also been a blessing.

Nicolae stands up and looks even more particularly annoyed when he checks the time on the flight board. He's afraid of flying, so he's always nervous.

"Well, brother", I say. "This is it. I wish you the very BEST of luck in Germany. I will see you in December, and I will show you Kurdistan. Trust me, you will love it."

Nicolae doesn't seem interested. Maybe he's worried about the plane crashing. You can tell when he's worried because he doesn't even speak or say anything funny, as he usually does. He pulls out his hand and shakes my hand confidently.

"It was good, Shawket", he says casually "but, you know, we'll see each other soon. Good luck on everything, and keep in touch with how everything is doing. Meanwhile, let's hope I don't die today".

And with that, he swiftly turned around and briskly walked away with his luggage, once again putting on that indifferent face as his headphones go in his ears and the sound of a loud plane leaving the airport fills the air.

Me and Nicolae, working on the book. He is
wearing the same football jersey that he wore when
I first met him. A few days later, he left for Berlin,
Germany to study for his Master's in International
Relations and Diplomacy.

A Brief History of Iraqi Kurdistan

Kurdistan is a region within the Middle East that extends territorially into four different countries: northern Kurdistan (southeast Turkey), Rojava (northern Syria), South Kurdistan (northern Iraq), and eastern Kurdistan (northwest Iran). The region where I was a born is part of the Iraqi Kurdistan. This part of Greater Kurdistan is the only autonomous region, controlled by the Kurdistan Regional Government. It must be kept in mind that the four regions of Kurdistan have had different types of histories and have been influenced by different types of governments and international bodies. It is primarily for this reason that there is sometimes infighting and disputes within these regions about how to approach certain issues.

From the ancient days to the Arabic Conquest of the area in about the seventh century a.d., Iraqi Kurdistan went through many stages. It is clear that much of the area is extremely fertile and mountainous, which enabled the people to be relatively safe from outside forces. In the early days, there appeared several city-states, and Erbil, our current capital city, seemed to be a thriving and important city back in 2100 B.C. This area was controlled by the Assyrians, and the area was known as Assyria, for a relatively long time. Many changes occurred and many empires managed to control the area as time went on. In 605 B.C., the area fell to the Neo-Babylonians and became part of the Athura Satrap (satrap means territory), which, at the time, was part of the Achaemenid Empire, known more famously today as the First Persian Empire.

Almost 300 years later, in the third century B.C., the Empire (and the territory), fell to Alexander the Great. It thereby became part of the Greek Seleucid Empire until 200 B.C. or so. It was about this time that the territory got a new name, Syria (which was a kind of Greek slang for Assyria). Afterwards, however, the territory came under Mithridates I of Parthia, and it soon developed into a semi-independent Kingdom of Adiabene. This lasted until about the first century B.C. The Romans came in not much later, and converted the area into Roman Assyria before the territory exchanged powers again with the Sasanian Empire of Persia. The territory became the Satrap of Assuristan, and this lasted almost 700 years until the Arabic Islamic Conquest.

When the Islam religion took hold of the Arab world in the seventh century, it spread rapidly in the Middle East. The fighting that began between the Arabs and the Kurds is what distinguishes the people of Kurdistan from the Arabs. They would come to identify themselves differently from those around them. Persia would see the end of its ancient glory and would collapse in exhaustion over centuries of war and conflict, and all its territories, including Iraqi Kurdistan, were split. Many of the territories changed hands between the Islamic Caliphates that soon emerged, and continued to be conquered and ruled by various empires, either the Persians, the Turks, or the Mongols. A jewel of pride for Kurdistan is that around this time there arose a man named Saladin, the great ruler of Egypt and Syria, who was a Kurd himself and who would become a European wonder for his victories and diplomacy. Iraqi Kurdistan was encompassed by three main principalities by the 16th Century: Baban, Badinan, and Soran. It was part of the Safavid Empire (considered by many to be the founding of the modern state of Iran). However, dispute over the land, and a constant back and forth control of the area between the Safavids and the Ottomans saw the Ottoman Empire come out on top. After the Treaty of Zuhad, the territory became Ottoman land, and it remained so, until World War I. In the 18th Century, however, the area was briefly controlled by Nader Shah of Iran until his death, whereas the Kurdish territories went back to Ottoman hands permanently.

World War I will be remembered by many people of the Middle East as a defining moment in the changing of the area. The British had defeated the Ottomans by the end of the war, and soon devoted their time trying to split the territories of the Middle East for themselves and their allies. Needless to say, various governments got their share, and turmoil arose when the Kurds were simply left out of the deal. The Treaty of Sevres, the document that outlined how the Ottoman Empire was to be portioned, was a complete disaster, leading to conflict in the region soon after its release. The treaty and impositions in it were extremely harsh, indeed, harsher than those found in the Treaty of Versailles targeting the Germans, and it was clear from the start that the winners of the world war had an irresistible desire to exploit the resources in the Middle East in the most economical way possible.

It was supremely unfortunate that the Kurds were ignored as an independent nation, as the British were concerned and rightly worried that if they allocated independence to the Kurds, the areas of Bagdad and Basra would rise up and demand their independence as well, a concern that certainly highlighted a conflict of interest. The British Empire wanted to control most of the

Mesopotamia region, and Kurdish independence threatened the stability and control of the region by the British Empire. As such, from 1919 onwards, revolts in the region were simply put down by the British through airstrikes, ground troops, and even chemical weapons. Revolutions arose and faded like a predictable wave in the ocean amidst the chaos. Every time a Kurdish resistance group arose claiming independence, the British were quick to quell the matter and ensure its control in the area. Mahmud Barzanji of Kurdistan revolted against the British several times, and he was given a chance to control the area to act as a buffer for the Turks who wanted to control the area. However, Barzanji was defiant and declared independence, whereas the Empire struck back and he was forced to hide in refuge as Kurdistan continued to get threatened and hit hard with the Empire's hard polices of containment.

After this, the Kurds continued to rebel, producing havoc in the area, demanding freedom and sovereignty, but were continuously ignored by the western powers, including the League of Nations. Uprising soon rose when the popular and central leader of the Iraqi Kurds called Mustafa Barzani continually challenged the Iraqi government. He demanded autonomy for the Kurds and would make constant deals with the Iraqi government to support this view. He supported Abd al-Karim Qasim, who was the Prime Minister of Iraq and supposedly one of the perpetrators of the Ba'ath Party coup that would soon see him gone. Qasim and Barzani made a deal whereas Qasim would recognize and support the Kurdish autonomy and show his support for Kurdistan as long as Barzani did the same towards his polices and government of Iraq. Unfortunately, this deal was not kept by Qasim, and the

Kurds continued to fight and rebel as Qasim turned on them with deadly force.

After a coup took power in Iraq, the new leader, Abdul Rahman Arif took control and continued to attack the Kurds. However, he ultimately lost, which led to his army being disintegrated at the Battle of Mount Handrin. Meanwhile, infighting between the Kurds on how to respond to the crisis led to an unstable Kurdistan, and the instability mainly resulted from the fighting factors, the urban Kurdish people and the Peshmerga (Freedom Fighters). An interplay of events occurred, where outside forces such as Iran and the Soviet Union, played a critical part in stalling the newly instituted Ba'ath party from gaining much control over the Kurds and their territory. Needless to say, a cooperation existed to allocate control, but the dicey effort on both sides of leadership led to continued conflict. However, by 1970, Iraqi Kurdistan gained autonomous sovereignty.

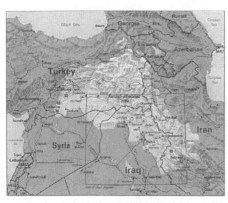

Greater Kurdistan

The Kurdish Inhabited Area as of 1992. Image Source: Perry-Castañeda Library Map Collection (University of Texas at Austin).

The United States secretly funded the Kurdish rebels with Iran's help in 1973. However, the Iraqi government took extreme measures to subdue the Kurds. Pushing the Kurds closer to Iran, they made what became infamously known as the Algerian Pact between Iran and Iraq, in which Iraq stated they would meet more Iranian demands if they stopped supplying the Kurds. After the agreement, rebellions arose in Iraq and the government took steep and extreme measures to squash them. The Iraqi government developed an Arabization program in which they deported hundreds of thousands of Kurds in Kurdistan and located them in areas where more Arabs lived and where they could learn the Arabic way. Hundreds of Kurdish villages were burnt to the ground. Chaos ensued everywhere. Many Kurds fled the country.

This process of Arabization is technically when my story begins. It was essentially a process of making the Kurds more Arab, which led to the Iraqi-Kurdish conflict. The Ba'ath Party developed a program to make us Kurds more modernized and like the Arabs, and it has led to many of us being killed and deported. Such process is often called "internal colonization". The extreme measures taken by Saddam Hussein and the Ba'ath Party caused such a panic that many of us fled the country. Essentially, I was in the middle of the Iraqi-Kurdish, and the sequence of the events that occurred from it.

The Iran-Iraq war started soon after, over territorial disputes and the chance for Iran to topple Saddam Hussein's regime. The war lasted about eight years and over a million people died in the process. Iraqi Kurdistan was heavily involved in this war, as well, and a huge civil war ensued in Iraq. It was around this time that Saddam Hussein began to use chemical weapons, and specifically targeted the Kurds. A plan was envisioned to be carried out by the dreaded Ali Hassan al-Majid, a cousin of Saddam, to eradicate the Kurds. Many Kurdish cities and villages were destroyed. Thousands of Kurdish people were killed instantly, with whole communities wiped out in a matter of a few hours. Instead of deporting the Kurds, the Kurdish areas were relocated with Arab people so as to infiltrate the Kurds and control what they did and how they lived. Many of the natural resources under Kurdish control were completely taken away and placed under Arab members, so as to ensure complete Iraqi control over the assets.

After the Persian Gulf War, outside Powers intervened to save and protect the Kurds. The United Nations declared a no-fly-zone over the Kurdish area, and Iraq withdrew forces by 1991, allowing for a relatively independent area. Ironically, though, Iraqi Kurdistan was extremely hurt economically because Saddam Hussein ordered a blockage against Kurdistan and the United Nations ordered a blockage against Iraq. The Kurdish economy nearly buckled under such strain, causing huge fighting between the two Kurdish parties, the Kurdish Democratic Party (KDP) and the Patriotic Union of Kurdistan (PUK). This fighting only made Kurdistan continually unstable, and it did more harm than good in undermining their cause. However, relations between Iraq and Kurdistan got much better as the years wore on, and economic prosperity began to rise in the region. Dohuk and Zakho became the most important cities at the time because these cities operated an illegal oil smuggling trade route to which was quite beneficial. Mutual collaboration between the Iraqi Kurds and Iraq soon developed on a limited level as Iraqi Kurdistan was becoming more and more independent.

The Iraq War began and the Kurds played a very pivotal role in helping take down the Iraqi regime. The Peshmerga helped the United States capture Saddam

Hussein, and helped the American troops in occupying Iraq, though they refused to advance into Bagdad because they wanted to keep away from the issues that have plagued Iraq since its conception. Since then, Iraqi Kurdistan has been given autonomy by the Iraqi constitution, though relations have been strained since 2008.

It must be noted that the Kurds extend outside the border of Iraq, so tensions arise because of outside interferences such as Turkey and Syria. Tensions broke out when Turkey militarily intervened in 2008, and reached its peak in 2012 when disputes arose between Iraq and Kurdistan over oil resources and territory. This has happened on and off throughout the years, and, as such, have caused many conflicts that have resulted in deaths and causalities. The recognition that Iraq is quickly collapsing as a state has encouraged both the Kurds and Turkey to start considering an independent Kurdistan. This seems highly plausible anyway because Iraqi Kurdistan is now naturally self-autonomous. It could self-sustain itself without the need for the Iraq government and its policies. The implication of such an action is a glory that has been anticipated for over 2,000 years.

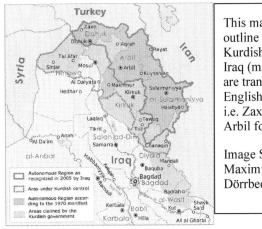

This map details the outline of the Kurdish region in Iraq (many words are translated into English equivalents, i.e. Zaxo for Zakho, Arbil for Erbil, etc.)

Image Source: Maximilian Dörrbecker, 2008

A referendum for session from Iraq has been anticipated for quite some time, since 2014. However, such action has been halted several times due to the current conflict in the region. Given the rapid expansion of ISIL, and the fact that the Kurds are primary fighters against them, the United States and other countries have been supportive in allocating resources to the Kurds in fighting ISIL on the ground. Thus, the fight against terror is often at the doorstep of the Kurdish people. We Kurds fight constantly for our self-preservation and independence.

On March 23, the President of the Iraqi Kurdistan, President Barzani, declared officially that a referendum would happen "before October" of 2016.

It is time, then, Kurdistan, to raise your voice. Being independent is not going to be easy, but we will move forward. Forever upward, high into the mountains, our voices will now be heard. We were always here, and we will always be, voices over the mountains.

Sources

The sources used for the information related in the "Brief History of Iraqi Kurdistan" was the Wikipedia page of *Kurdistan* and *Iraqi Kurdistan.*

Further information was gathered from "A People Without a Country: The Kurds and Kurdistan" by Gérard Chaliand and the "Miracle of the Kurds" by Stephen Mansfield.

Made in the USA
Middletown, DE
03 November 2019

77906516R00046